How to Meet No One

UNION SQUARE & CO.
NEW YORK

Union Square & Co. and the distinctive Union Square & Co. logo are trademarks of Sterling Publishing Co., Inc.

Union Square & Co., LLC, is a subsidiary of Sterling Publishing Co., Inc.

ISBN 978-1-4549-5826-0

For information about custom editions, special sales, and premium purchases, please contact specialsales@unionsquareandco.com.

Printed in China

2 4 6 8 10 9 7 5 3 1

unionsquareandco.com

Cover and interior design by Tracy Sunrize

How to Meet No One

an introvert's guide to surviving a world filled with people

Ainsley Drew

@lousydrawingsforgoodpeople

UNION SQUARE & CO.
NEW YORK

You're not the only one who feels this way.

Interacting with the world is difficult. For decades I've bumbled through "normal life" having nothing more than my internal screaming and cursory sense of manners to keep me from being 5150'd for my entire adulthood. Through posting my lousy drawings on the internet, I've found that I'm not alone, and there's a whole legion of us introverts enduring social expectations with a chorus of "What's wrong with me?" echoing through our heads.

Guess what? There's nothing wrong with you. It's okay to hate parties. You're not weird for not wanting to chitchat. Your awkward interactions aren't proof that you were dropped off on this planet by aliens as a baby. You're not alone in wanting to be alone.

Ideally, you're reading this in the privacy of your own space, happily withdrawn from the world. But if not, hopefully this book will be a stop sign for anyone looking for small talk. It's written for you, to remind you that your quirks aren't a curse and that we introverts can be inclusive while remaining reclusive. Happy isolating!

The worst thing about waking up is knowing you have to leave the house.

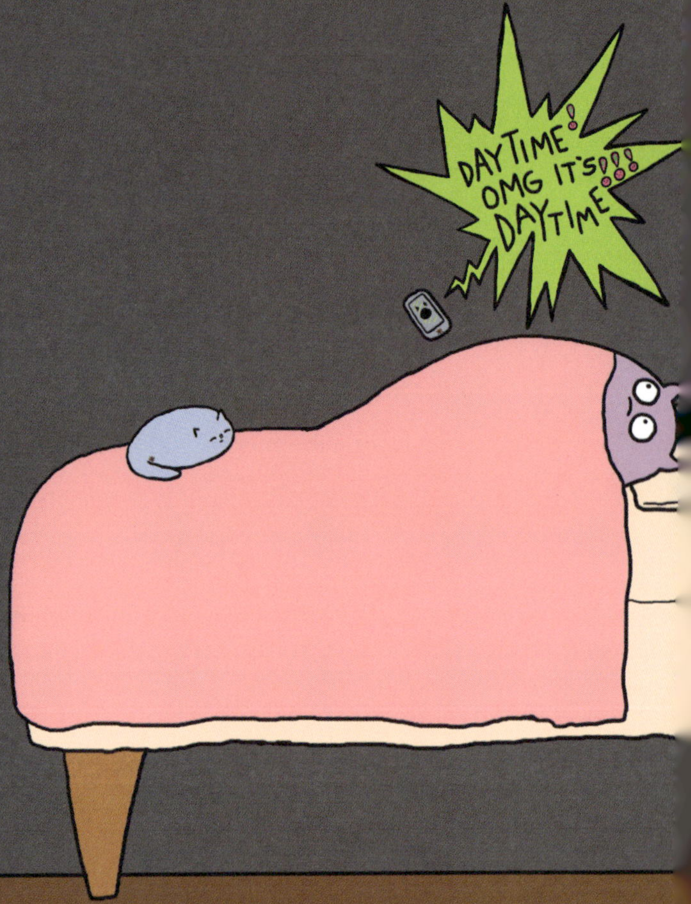

UUUGH... I DON'T WANNA GO TO WORK...

We all get burnt out or overstimulated by different things. Only you know what sets you off.

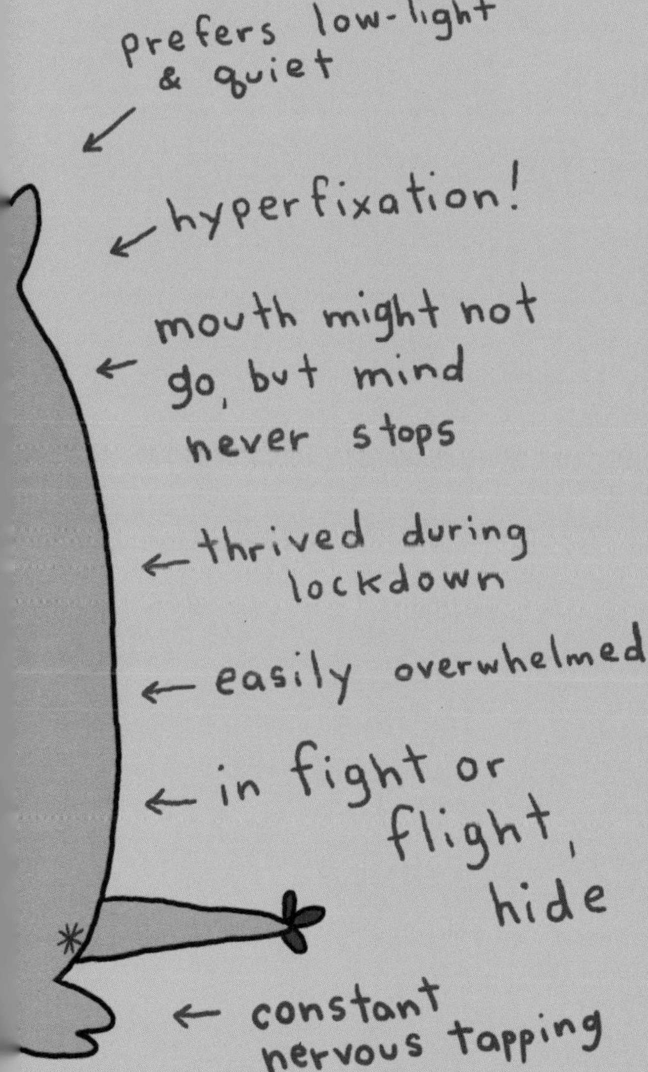
prefers low-light & quiet
hyperfixation!
mouth might not go, but mind never stops
thrived during lockdown
easily overwhelmed
in fight or flight, hide
constant nervous tapping

Until everything is automated to the point that we don't have to interact with one another, we all have to obsess about how we present in public.

pretty
busy & important
too cool
XPENSIV
COFFEE

PRO TIP!
ALWAYS BRING US WITH YOU!
...even if we're not charged!

WARNING! IF YOUR PHONE ISN'T ON SILENT MODE IT MIGHT RING!!!
PRO TIP! IF YOU'VE FORGOTTEN YOUR EARBUDS, PRETEND YOU'RE ON THE PHONE!
(↑ THIS ACTUALLY HAPPENED TO ME...)

When being in public becomes overwhelming, try the technique known as 5-4-3-2-1, which might break the relentless loop of terror playing in your head.

1.
am I going to throw up???
2. coffee... is that too obvious?
do I smell pee?
3.
Hall & Oates on speaker
that guy coughing (cover your mouth!)
who is swallowing so loud?
4.
sweaty hands
gotta pee?
itchy tag
are my socks wet?
5:
really bright fluorescent light
sticky stain on floor
booger wiped on wall
that girl looking at me (why?)
is that a piercing...???

DO YOU HAVE A REUSABLE MUG FOR THE "SAVE THE EARTH, SAVE YOURSELF" DISCOUNT?
UM, I'M SORRY I PROMISE...I USUALLY DO TODAY I FORGOT MINE AT HOME BUT I SWEAR I LOVE EARTH...
XPENSIV COFFEE

WOULD YOU LIKE TO DONATE ONE DOLLAR TO THE SICK & DYING CUTE PUPPIES FOUNDATION WITH YOUR PURCHASE TODAY?
NO, I MEAN, I CAN'T, BUT I WANT TO. PUPPIES ARE THE BEST. I'M JUST BROKE!
XPENSIV COFFEE
XPENSIV
COFFEE

WOULD YOU LIKE A RECEIPT?
YOU TOO!
XPENSIV
COFFEE

I WILL OBSESS ABOUT THIS FOR THE REST OF THE DAY
"WOULD YOU LIKE A RECEIPT?"
"YOU TOO!"

If you see someone from your past, hide.

No matter how much you need it, never ask for help.
Asking for help means talking to strangers.
If you can't find the bathroom, just keep looking.
If you can't reach something, you didn't really need it anyway.

WHAT DO I DO WITH MY HANDS?
DID I SWALLOW TOO LOUD?
WHAT'S MY FACE DOING?
PRO TIP! YOU DON'T HAVE TO WORRY ABOUT HOW THE WORLD PERCEIVES YOU. EVERYBODY IS ONLY WORRIED ABOUT THEMSELVES.

HOW NOT TO HAVE SMALL TALK
(former neighbor, three years removed)

When you spot someone from a past life, pray that they are as unwilling to engage in small talk as you are.

But be prepared—they may be one of those creepy-weirdo friendly folk who won't pick up what you're putting down.

If they insist on engaging with you, remember that any awkwardness that ensues is on them.

Elevator etiquette:

If we're going to be stuck in this tin can together, at least be quiet.

If you've worn deodorant: thank you.

If you've worn "nice" cologne: may both sides of your pillow be warm when you flip it.

If you insist on talking, with your
hot breath unwelcome on my neck:

may your day be cursed
from here on out.

EFFECTIVE METHODS FOR AVOIDING CUBICLE TALK
1: HIDE.

2. FEIGN OVERLOAD.

WHATCHYA DOIN' THIS WEEKEND?

3. BE YOUR WEIRD, WEIRD SELF.

BREAKDOWN IN THE BREAK ROOM

(ways to cope at work)

THIEVES WILL BE STAPLED TO THE WALL
KIM'S CHI
VINEGAR JUICE
STEVE'S MILK
ROB
DON'T EVEN THINK
NOPE
NOT YOUR SOUP
JJ
ALEX'S
CHUNK O' CHEESE
AVOID CONFLICT: ALWAYS LABEL YOUR FOOD

MAXIMIZE YOUR BREAK

Boss makes a dollar,
I make a dime,
that's why I poop
on company time.

Since you can't avoid your boss, pretend you're approachable!

Have two or three questions at the ready, especially if they include bougie hobbies like yachting or polo!

HEY, SOME OF US ARE GONNA GO GET PIZZA...
ALWAYS IRISH GOODBYE

SOCIAL SETTINGS
HOW DOES ANYBODY DO THIS??

EVERYBODY LOVES A
PARTY!

HOW TO SPOT
the CLOSE TALKER
blahblah
blah blahblah
blah BLAH
blahblah
BLAH BLAH
BLAH
blah blah blah
blahblah blah
blah blahblah
blahblah
BLAH
blah

AN EXTROVERT
the loud mouth
the pushy one
HEY! EVERYONE! YOU HAVE TO TRY MY HOMEMADE GORGONZOLA & GEFILTE FISH BALLS!
the drama queen

EXTROVERTED SIGNS
LEO
(melodramatic)
YOU HAVE FOOD IN YOUR TEETH
SAGITTARIUS
(half brutally honest, half horse)
ARIES
(Stabby)

INTROVERTED SIGNS
PISCES
doo dooo doo...
(in their own world)
CANCER
(softy)
SCORPIO
(sociopath)

WHY IS IT CALLED HAPPY HOUR?
THIS GUY IS SUCH A LOSER. HOW DOES HE HAVE A BETTER JOB THAN ME?
WHERE'S THE BATHROOM? I CAN POST A TIK TOK FROM THE TOILET...
404 FILE NOT FOUND

WHEN NO ONE IS HAPPY?
AM I THE HOTTEST ONE HERE? I SHOULD BE THE HOTTEST ONE HERE.
THWUMP!
HAHA *hic!* AHAHAHA

At mandatory work gatherings that force you to be social, remember: don't overshare!

I HAVE A CAT NAMED STEVE.

Try to find
common interests!
DO YOU LIKE TAYLOR SWIFT?

IS THAT THE GUY WHO SINGS I'VE SEEN FIRE & I'VE SEEN RAIN...?

TiP! When all else fails . . . start screaming.

LUG BEER
AAAAAAAP

This works for flirting, too!

AAAAAA

How to deal with being hit on . . .

LET'S MAKE IT WEIRD...

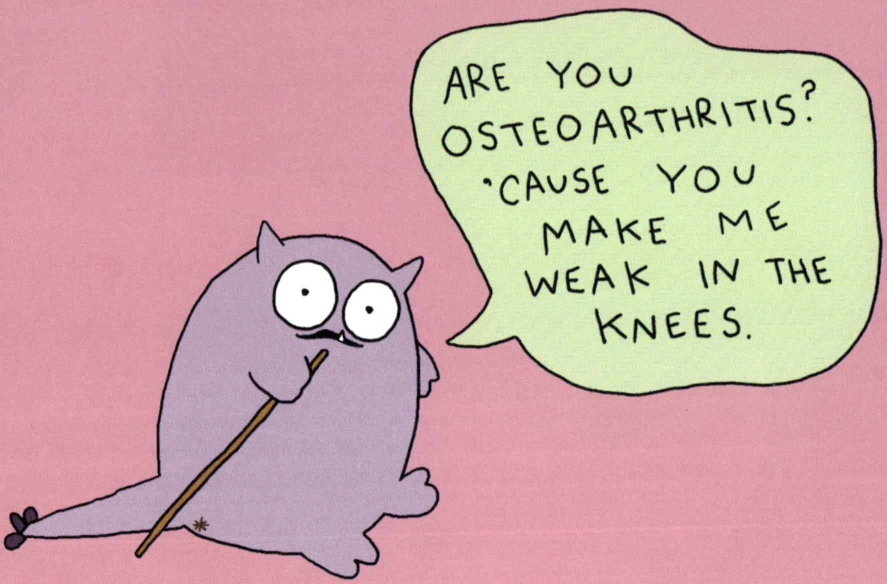
ARE YOU OSTEOARTHRITIS? 'CAUSE YOU MAKE ME WEAK IN THE KNEES.

DO YOU WORK FOR NASA? 'CAUSE THAT BUTT IS OUT OF THIS WORLD.

IS YOUR FATHER A BEAVER? 'CAUSE DAAAMN!

HOW TO AVOID NON-CONSENSUAL TOUCH

CHOMP!

Embrace being ghosted.

Not everyone wants a partner.

Some of us just want some space.

HOW TO SURVIVE SOCIAL SITUATIONS

TiP! Go nonverbal!

HOW "NORMAL" PEOPLE CAN PERCEIVE QUIET PEOPLE
BROODING
IF ONLY I HAD SOMETHING TO SAY...
SEXY
EUROPEAN
MYSTERIOUS
COUGH! HACK!

TiP!
Take over tasks that require little interaction!
CLEANING!
... THANKS! ... SO THEN I SAID...
mhm
SERVING!
PARKING CARS!

. . . and find the most accommodating people to hang out with.
BABIES!
SENIOR CITIZENS!
whaa?
PETS!

BABY SHOWER
Same.
WWAAAAAAAH

How to avoid social settings *before* they occur:

Invites?

Always RSVP "no"

'cause if you RSVP "yes,"
you're gonna wanna cancel.

RSVP etiquette:

Always send a gift that arrives before your “will not attend” guilt does.

True friends of introverts know
the joy of canceled plans
and the quiet hang.

Divorced parents
are a boon for holidays.

If your parents are still together,
make up a job or a fake partner that
you have to go see instead!

Your time off is

YOURS.

You're allowed to say no!

And you can always feign sickness if being honest seems impossible.

Be direct with extroverts.

Or use them to your advantage.

For example, someone neurotypical can make phone appointments for you.

TiP at the gym! Fly your freak flag and make sure you have access to your desired equipment.

TiP at the DMV!

Stay quietly miserable like everyone else!

And make sure you have a buffer in situations where being grumpy or weird won't prevent interactions.

THIS IS LITERALLY MY NIGHTMARE.

TiP for when you can't escape!

Pretend you don't know how to speak any language.

A message to dental hygienists:
Whether or not your patient is an introvert, we

CANNOT RESPOND TO YOU

with sharp things in our mouths.

When small talk is unavoidable,
know at least a bit about celebrity gossip.

Or just stay quiet.
You don't owe anyone an explanation.

SUBSCRIBE
DON'T GO IN THE COMMENTS. EVER.
Technology can be a landmine— avoid it at all costs.
AS PER MY LAST EMAIL...
YOU HAVE 40 MESSAGES
TECH NO!
HOORAY FOR FILTERS, SPAM, & THE DELETE BUTTON
IF YOU DON'T CHECK IT, IT DOESN'T EXIST
DMs
hiiii
;)
s'up

Homeward bound:

you're almost there!

Always avoid your neighbors,
lest they think you want to chat every time you see them.

When it comes to the stairwells, mailbox, or elevators, timing is everything!

Living alone is the dream,
but being able to afford it often isn't reality.

How to be a roommate:
Be civil enough to avoid conflict, be scarce enough to avoid conversation, and try to avoid getting mad at the filth.

Pretend to be cool with things you hate.

Open all bills promptly
and pay exactly the amount you owe.

And never, ever answer the door.

Make sure you have a place
where you can retreat.

If living with your family, focus on the positives.

no rent

free food

laundry services

support system

YOU GAVE ME THE FLU!
NO, YOU GAVE ME THE FLU!

And if you’re cohabitating, remember that you love them . . .

. . . and don't be afraid to ask for what you need in a living arrangement.

And set firm boundaries.

IDEALLY, SAVE YOUR MONEY, SELL YOUR STUFF, AND FIND A PLACE WHERE YOU CAN LIVE ALONE.
HEY! WHAT ABOUT ME?!

Tip! Just become nocturnal!

Being awake when nobody else is means that you don't have to see anybody. And it's reasonable not to text back at 2:00 a.m.

Built-in excuse!

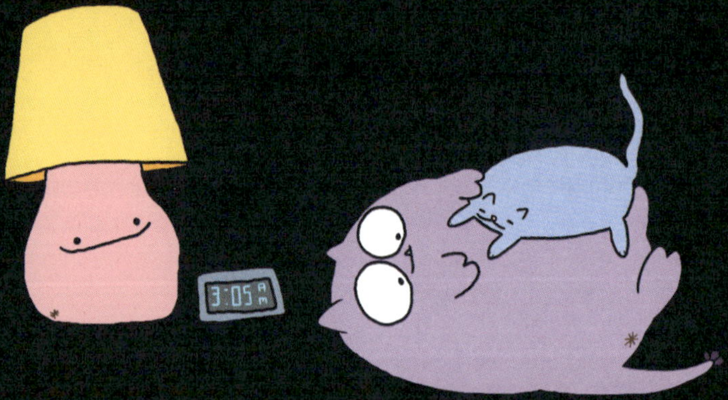

If you are lucky enough to live alone, set up your apartment to make sure you stay that way.

DON'T LET YOUR BRAIN RUIN A GOOD TIME
YIKES!

Negative self-talk can sabotage solitude,
so maintain healthy habits to protect your peace.

Try repeating mantras!

Journal about your feelings!

Put your phone on Do Not Disturb.

Seek professional help, if need be.

Make sure your needs are met.

YUM
O'S

Relish your time alone.
You spend the most time with yourself,
so you might as well enjoy it!

UGGHH... WORK TOMORROW...
I DON'T WORK!
knead knead...

Uh-oh. It's the end of the book.

That means you're going to have to start interacting with people again. Maybe we can just shove a bunch of extra blank pages back here so you can pretend you're still reading?

If you are like me, it's hard to exist in a world that prioritizes socializing, partnering up, and managing personalities in real life and online. Hopefully you feel a little less different after reading this book. You're not canceling plans by yourself! There are millions of recluses just like you who are seething at the idea of that meeting tomorrow, or struggling with how they're going to get through that second date.

If you feel seen, I'm glad. If you feel like you understand your standoffish friend or family member as the result of these doodles, hooray! The only thing I strive for is to make people smile, whether it's among a crowd or by themselves. So don't reach out! Be a stranger! And most of all, enjoy your time alone.

To JJ, for never saying "no." I love you more than I can express, but I'll keep trying. You're the best partner I could ever ask for. I'm yours forever.

To Dinah Dunn and the entire team at Indelible Editions, thank you for taking a chance on me. Being an author on your squad is beyond my wildest dreams.

To Jay Sacher and everyone at Union Square, including Tracy Sunrize, Lisa Forde, and Christine Borris, your patience is limitless. Thank you for allowing so much creative freedom and for giving me a shot.

Dad, I finally did something! Sorry it took so long.

Carey and Jake, I love you. Thanks for breaking the stepmom and stepbrother tropes.

To the Drews, thanks for not disowning me. I'm sure it was difficult at times. I love you all.

Thank you to Jonathan Jarrett; Lance Curran and Threadless; Elliott Kalan; Bean; Captain Eyeliner for being my Tyler Durden; Esther Lin for the punchfaces and inspiring the grind; Jordan Tek (aka I. JORDAN), whose music and kindness know no bounds; Tara Collins for going beyond experience, strength, and hope; everyone who follows, messages, lurks, likes, and shares; every odd kid wondering what they're doing . . . you matter. Be weird. Make stuff. I love you.

Oh, and to my cats,
you can totally eat my corpse.